I'M FINE

by

Rose Gibson

Published by Mabel and Stanley Publishing

September 2025

I'M FINE

The truth about becoming a mum (that no one warns you about)

This book is for every woman who's ever looked around and thought,

How did I end up here?

Blending heartfelt storytelling with laugh-out-loud honesty, this book journeys through the roller coaster of life as a mother, the hormonal highs and lows, the identity shifts, the mental load, the invisible (and visible) labour and the unspoken feelings we're told we shouldn't feel but absolutely do.

This isn't a manual. It's a mirror. It's not about fixing yourself. It's about seeing yourself clearly, kindly and with the honesty you'd give your best friend after a glass of wine and a long cry.

With interactive prompts throughout to help you untangle the noise in your head and reconnect with the *you* beneath the chaos of being a mum, this book gives you permission to feel it all and maybe even let some of it go.

And you don't have to do it alone.

WHY THIS BOOK?

“I'm fine.”

It's what women say when we're not. When we're drowning in mental load, stuck between the person we were and the mother we're still becoming, when we're holding it all together with caffeine, cracked mascara and a colour-coded calendar.

I'm Fine is a raw, relatable and honest exploration of modern womanhood and all the invisible roles we never signed up for but somehow ended up carrying.

It's part memoir, part manifesto, part mirror, a space where women can finally admit:

I love my children but I'm exhausted. I wanted this life but I didn't expect it to feel like this.

Drawing on personal stories and real conversations, this book unpacks everything we're told not to talk about. The identity crisis of motherhood, the hormonal roller coaster, the resentment, the mental list that never ends and the pressure to do it all without ever losing your cool.

So, why this book?

With interactive pages and a voice that feels more like a best friend than a self-help guru, I'm Fine gives women permission to feel it all and to realise they're not broken, just burdened.

We're in an epidemic of burnout. Because women are nodding politely through parenting books but secretly Googling, *why am I crying in the Aldi car park again?* Because there's power in saying the quiet parts out loud.

This isn't a guide to being better.

It's an invitation to be honest.

"The only book you need, it feels like a best friend in a book."

Contents

INTRODUCTION

Hey Mama, I'm Rose.

If you're holding this book, chances are you're somewhere on the wild ride that is motherhood, maybe you're pregnant, maybe the baby's already here or maybe you're just trying to figure out where *you* went while trying to keep a small human alive. Either way, I want to start by saying this:

You're not doing it wrong.

You're not broken.

And you are absolutely not alone.

This book was born from the very real, very messy, very emotional trenches of many women who have walked the path before you.

I remember standing in the middle of the living room, baby on one hip, cold coffee in the other hand, Googling *is it normal to feel like I've lost myself?* If that sounds familiar, I see you.

What no one really told me (and maybe no one told you either) is that while everyone's busy prepping for the birth, very few people prepare you for what happens after. The stuff that's not on the Instagram reels or the cute milestone cards. The truth about bleeding nipples, crying in the bath when your nether regions are on fire, your relationship taking a sideways step or suddenly not recognising your own reflection. But also, the quiet moments when you do recognise her again, stronger, softer, more powerful than ever.

This is your prewarning that this book is a no filter, no fluff guide written for women like us, women who want to feel seen, supported and empowered. Not just as mums, but as whole human beings. It's conversational because we don't need more clinical leaflets. It's real because pretending everything's fine on social media doesn't help anyone. It's interactive because *your* voice and *your* story matter too.

Inside, you'll find chapters you can read in any order, practical prompts to reconnect with your body and mind and honest reflections that say all the things your antenatal class probably didn't.

My goal? That you feel less alone. That you laugh out loud. That you maybe cry (a little). And that you walk away feeling just a bit more *you* again.

Motherhood doesn't come with a manual but if it did, I'd want it to sound something like this.

You've got this.

And I've got you.

With love,

Rose

FYI on how to use this book, whether you have the paper version or the e-book, there are practical tools, pages and prompts after every chapter.

Use them as you will.

If you've never put pen to paper about yourself sometimes it can feel weird, kind of like when you first feel your baby wiggling in your womb…but that weirdness soon becomes awesome and empowering.

Maybe you're a doodler or a note scribbler. You do *you*. There is no right and no wrong.

You don't need to share this book with anyone but it will help you clarify your feelings and your inner beliefs as you work through each chapter.

CHAPTER ONE

It's normal to feel overwhelmed (Even if you *wanted this* so badly)

So let's get this out of the way straight away…

You *can* love your baby and still feel like you're drowning.

You *can* be so grateful and still want to scream into a pillow.

You *can* be doing your absolute best and still feel like you're failing.

That wave of emotions? That's not weakness. That's not you doing it wrong.

That's called overwhelm, and it's one of the most common (yet least talked about) parts of early motherhood.

So what *is* overwhelm, really?

Overwhelm is what happens when your brain and body are being asked to do too much, too fast, for too long. It's a full-body signal that you've hit capacity.

Here's the science-y bit, but don't worry, I'll keep it short.

When you have a baby, your brain is flooded with hormones like oxytocin (the love hormone) and prolactin (milk production), whilst also dealing with sleep deprivation, constant decision making and huge emotional shifts.

Add to that:

- Recovery from birth (whether vaginal or c-section).
- Changes in your relationship dynamics.
- A crying, completely dependent tiny human.
- Pressure to *bounce back*.
- And, oh yeah, trying to remember who *you* even are.

Suddenly, your nervous system is on red alert. You're not broken. You're just human. And you've got a lot going on.

What overwhelm might look like:

- Crying for *no reason* (there is a reason by the way, your nervous system is fried).
- Feeling like you can't make even the smallest decisions (hello, decision fatigue).
- Snapping at people you love, then feeling guilty about it.
- Wanting to run away and also never leave your baby.
- Feeling anxious, numb, on edge, foggy or all of the above.

Sound familiar? That's overwhelm. And it doesn't mean you're not coping. It means you need space, support and a slower pace.

One of the most damaging myths we're fed as women is that we should be able to *handle it all*.

Here's the truth.

You weren't meant to do this alone.

You weren't meant to do this perfectly.

And you definitely weren't meant to do it silently.

Ever heard the saying, *It takes a village to raise a child*? It's not just a cute quote, it's a deeply rooted truth. Because once upon a time, that's exactly how it was. Villages, tribes, communities, they all rallied around new mothers. They brought food, watched the babies while you slept, shared wisdom passed down through generations and made sure no woman was navigating this alone.

But today? We've got WhatsApp chats and white noise machines.

We've got Google at 3am and *you got this, mama!* captions on Instagram…but often, we don't actually feel like anyone's really got us. Our 'villages' are scattered, busy and let's be honest sometimes non-existent.

We've created a culture that praises independence and quiet suffering. Where asking for help feels like failure and showing struggle gets a side eye or silence.

But you, my beautiful Mama, you are not weak for needing rest and support, you're human.

Strong women aren't the ones who never need help. They're the ones who know when to whisper, "I can't do this alone", even if their voice shakes.

They're the ones who start again, even when the sink's full, the washing's piled up, and no one's cheered for them in weeks.

This book? It's a little slice of that village.

It's one voice in your corner saying, '*you're not alone*', even if it feels like it today.

Because raising a baby is huge. Becoming a mother is bigger.

And doing both without a support system? Practically impossible. Let's stop pretending we have to do it all, all the time.

Let's rebuild that village, one honest conversation at a time. No wonder we are overwhelmed and overwhelm is your body waving a flag saying:

Hey, I need rest. I need care. I need time.

You are not a machine. You don't need to *power through* this.

You're allowed to rest.

You're allowed to ask for help.

You're allowed to not love every moment.

Overwhelm might show up.

But so will your strength.

And if you're screaming at me through the pages, *'But how do I rest? How do I ask for help when I don't even know what I need?* keep going.

I hear you. I am you. And I promise, I won't just leave you here feeling seen but stuck.

The next chapters will offer you practical tools, real things, not fluffy nonsense, to help you move forward. But first, you have to be honest about where you are now.

There will be days where you can't rest, where someone's always poorly, the house is upside down, work won't stop pinging and your body aches in a way that sleep alone can't fix.

There will be days where you feel so deeply bored, touched out and tired of being needed.

Sit with those days.

I don't have a magic wand to wave you out of them, I wish I did.

But I do have these pages. Use them. Use the prompts, the exercises, the space in between to make sense of what you're carrying and where you might gently put some of it down.

This is just chapter one.

Stick with me.

RIGHT NOW, WHAT AM I FEELING?

Do these pages at your own pace. Come back to them another time if they feel too much right now. There is no pressure to do them if they're not for you...you do you!

WHAT AM I HOLDING THAT I CAN LET GO OF (EVEN JUST FOR TODAY)?

NOTES

SAY SOMETHING KIND

SOMETHING I WOULD SAY TO SOMEONE ELSE	NOW TO MYSELF
You look lovely in that outfit.	I feel confident and comfortable in my clothes today.

What is currently taking up space in your head? (to-do lists, emotions, mental clutter... let it spill out)

CHAPTER TWO

You are enough, even when you feel like you're not

Do you have a cold cup of tea somewhere in the house and a thousand tabs open in your brain?

Let's just pause for a second. Breathe in…and out.

Now hear this:

You are enough.

Not just on the days when everything goes right.

Not only when the baby sleeps.

Not only when you've managed to make it to a class, prep a meal, and not cry during CBeebies bedtime story.

You are enough exactly as you are.

Because here's the sneaky lie we've been sold: that you have to be doing more, being more or giving more to be a *good mum*. That if you're not soaking up every second with some serene glow, you're doing it wrong. That if you don't bounce back with a flat stomach and colour-coded weaning chart, you're falling short.

That if you ask for help, whether it's five minutes to shower, or someone to hold the baby while you drink your lukewarm cuppa, you're weak.

It's utter nonsense.

And yet…the pressure sticks. It shows up when your baby's crying in the middle of the supermarket and you feel all the eyes burning holes in your back. It whispers when you're rocking your baby at 2am, 3am, 4am, wondering if anyone else feels this lost.

It screams when you scroll social media and see some mum looking flawless with a baby who apparently naps on schedule and eats homemade organic sweet potato mash.

The truth is, people can be mean. They can be judgmental.

Sometimes, they'll look at you sideways when your toddler is mid tantrum in aisle four, or when your pushchair takes up too much room on the bus or when you're in your third day of dry shampoo.

Raise your chin. Stand tall. Give them your best dazzling, too tired to care, full of inner strength smile.

Let them.

Let them think what they want. Because you know the truth. You're there, doing the invisible, emotional, unglamorous work that no one sees but that matters more than anything.

So when they give you that side eye? You give them your best superwomen dazzling smile back.

The kind that says,

I'm not here to be perfect. I'm here to be real. And I'm doing my best. That is more than enough.

Here's a challenge for you…talk to yourself the same way you'd talk to a friend.

You wouldn't tell her she's failing because she's tired.

You wouldn't shame her for needing rest.

You wouldn't tell her she's not enough because her house is a mess or she's Googling *can toddlers survive on raisins?*

So why speak to yourself that way?

Let's change the script. Let's rewrite the voice in your head.

Let me tell you about the time I nearly combusted over a kitchen full of half-eaten cereal and laundry.

I was in that glamorous era with a toddler and a baby (I think about 2014) outfit combo of slightly stretched Primark leggings and oversized jumper. It was a normal weekday. My mum said she'd pop over. Great, she'd seen my unfiltered life before, no biggie.

What she didn't mention was that she was bringing my Gran and Aunty along for the ride. Now, my extended family are people who live over an hour away. People who don't just casually drop by.

Usually, I'd do the classic throw everything into the cupboard under the stairs routine, spritz a bit of Zoflora in the air and fake domestic goddess.

But this time? No warning. No prep. So naturally, my internal panic alarm went off like a foghorn. I was a deer in the headlights standing in a kitchen of shame, breakfast still on the table, laundry piles like small mountains and a general sense of baby apocalypse.

I felt mortified.

And here's the real clincher: they didn't even care. Not one bit. They cooed over my baby boy, chatted away, and didn't bat an eyelid at the mess. But I cared. Deeply. I felt like I'd failed some invisible motherhood standard that says, *you must be put together at all times or you're doing it wrong.*

It took me a long time to get to the point where I could say, "I don't care. I can't do it all. If you're judging, that's on you. I'm doing my best."

And mama, I wish someone had told me this sooner.

So here it is, from me to you…You're enough.

Just as you are.

Right now.

HOW HAVE I SPOKEN TO MYSELF TODAY?

Go on.... Give it a try... What have you said to yourself?

REWRITE IT HOW I WOULD SAY IT TO MY BESTIE!

Be as kind to yourself as you would to others!

NEGATIVE V POSITIVE

Use this circle to write down any negative words you say to yourself

Use this circle to reframe those words into something positive

Your inner voice is still you.
Be kind to her, she is powerful and beautiful.

CHAPTER THREE

'Mum Guilt' is a liar

The voice that creeps in at 3am, whispers while you scroll Instagram and chimes in every time you try to do something for you.

You know the one:

You didn't play enough today.

You fed them freezer food again?

You should really enjoy every second.

Yeah. That voice? That's Mum Guilt, and it's a lying little gremlin.

Guilt is supposed to be a signal, a gentle nudge when we've actually done something wrong. But 'mum guilt' is often just the echo of unrealistic expectations. It's society's pressure, the highlight reels we compare ourselves to, the generations of *perfect* mothers we think we're failing to live up to.

You feel guilty for working.

You feel guilty for staying home.

You feel guilty for craving time alone…and also guilty for not enjoying every second together.

It's exhausting.

And it's unfair.

You even feel guilty asking for help, especially from the people who already do so much. The grandparents who babysat last week, your partner who's just come off a long shift, the friend who says, "any time" but you still hesitate.

You sit there, texting and deleting, convincing yourself you should be able to handle it on your own. That everyone else is managing.

That you'd be a burden. Guilt is not proof that you're failing; it's often a sign that you care, you literally care so much that you feel guilty about it! That you're constantly weighing up what's best.

But let's get one thing straight: you *are* allowed to meet your own needs without apology.

I have a mug that one of my clients got me for Christmas, and it says, '*you cannot pour from an empty cup*'. Taking care of yourself isn't selfish, it's essential.

So when guilt starts whispering again, ask yourself…is this coming from my values or from pressure to be everything to everyone?

Then kindly tell guilt to jog on. You've got more important things to focus on, like being a real, loving, imperfect mum. And that is more than enough.

WHAT HAVE I FELT GUILTY ABOUT?

I have started you off on the next page with my personal guilt gremlin... now reframe it to what it ACTUALLY is!

NOW REFRAME IT

I feel guilty for putting the TV on for an hour so I can drink a hot coffee.	I need a break, my children get a break too. We will both benefit and nothing bad will happen.

THOUGHTS

WRITE DOWN EVERYTHING MY INNER GREMLIN SAYS ON A HARD DAY

Let it speak without filter!

Mum guilt is a liar. You're doing better than you think.

Use this space to be honest with yourself. Guilt grows in silence. By naming it, you take away its power.

CHAPTER FOUR

You might not bond right away (and you're still a good mum)

Literally no right or wrong!

You might not feel that magical, movie-scene rush of love the second your baby is placed on your chest. And if that's you, if you're blinking through the exhaustion, slightly numb, slightly terrified, thinking, *Wait...am I supposed to feel something more than this?* I want you to know something very, very important.

You are still a good mum.

We've been sold this one version of initial bond, tearfulness, swells of love, and immediate connection like the final scene of a romcom. But the reality? For many of us, strong bonds don't arrive in a cinematic moment; it builds. It brews. It sometimes takes days, weeks, even months.

And that is completely normal.

You've just run a marathon (aka labour), or maybe you were wheeled into surgery and are healing from a major operation. Your hormones are crashing like a wave on Scarborough beach. You're sore, confused and suddenly responsible for a brand-new tiny mini human. That's a lot to process.

Add in sleep deprivation, physical recovery, feeding challenges, and a body that doesn't feel like yours anymore…and yeah, instant fairy tale rushes might not be your first emotional response.

That does not mean there's something wrong with you. You might be in survival mode.

You also might be grieving your old life a bit. You might just be adjusting. That makes you human.

Think about the relationships you've had in life, your partner, friends even family. Most of them took time to grow. Why would we expect anything different with the tiny stranger who just showed up and turned your world upside down?

It doesn't have to feel warm and fuzzy immediately. Sometimes, it feels like showing up and doing the hard thing again and again, until one day you look at them and realise, *Oh wow…there you are. And here I am. And I love you.*

Do not compare your beginning to someone else's highlight reel. The mum on Instagram with the dreamy filter and caption about instant love? She might be feeling lost inside, too.

Social media is not the full story. Your story is unfolding in its own beautiful, sometimes messy way.

If the feelings of disconnect don't ease, or you feel persistently numb, anxious or overwhelmed or you're even a tiny bit unsure, talk to someone.

Your midwife. Your health visitor. Your GP. Postnatal mental health is real and you deserve support.

You don't have to white knuckle your way through this.

WHEN HAVE I FELT MOST CONNECTED TO MY BABY?

Maybe it was the way they looked at you, the weight of them sleeping on your chest or just breathing in rhythm.

WHAT DO I WISH BONDING LOOKED LIKE?

WHERE MIGHT I BE PLACING PRESSURE ON MYSELF?

WHAT DO I FEEL WHEN I HOLD MY BABY?

WHAT DO I FEEL WHEN I SMELL MY BABY?

Use this space to note down the small connections you feel with your baby.

CHAPTER FIVE

You won't be the same, but that's not a bad thing

Standing in front of the hospital mirror after a c-section, I remember the moment it hit me.

I was in one of those strange hospital shower rooms, half toilet, half washing cubicle, definitely not made with dignity in mind. I stood there in the world's worst post-surgery nappy pants, my dressing half peeled off, staring at myself in the mirror.

I had just had a c-section. I looked at the reflection staring back at me and thought, *Oh my gosh…is this the new me?*

I used to be a dancer. A fitness teacher. I'd always felt strong and sure of myself in both body and mind. But standing there, post op, with my abdominal muscles soft and my womb empty, I didn't feel strong; I felt like I was grieving. Like I had to suddenly become someone else, and I wasn't ready for that.

No one had prepared me for this part. No one talked about the grief of who you were before. I didn't have mum friends. I was 22, holding a tiny baby in my arms, but feeling like I had completely lost me.

I wanted her, my beautiful daughter, but I also wanted *me.*

The *me* who could do push ups without wincing. The *me* who recognised her reflection.

The *me* who felt in control.

Instead, I stood there, panic tightening my chest, naked in a hospital bathroom with a dodgy lock, praying no one walked in because I could not take that level of vulnerability on top of everything else.

That was the first time I realised just how alone I felt. How changed I was. Not just physically but in every single way.

But here's the thing, and some people take a lifetime to work this out, change isn't bad. It's scary, yes. Messy, often. But bad? No.

You probably won't go back to the *old you.*

As I've gotten older, that version of me, the one who panicked in the hospital mirror, has stayed with me. Not as someone I lost, but as a part of who I became. A woman who evolved. Who grew stronger. Who learned to say, "This is me now and she's worthy too."

Change whispered, *we've got you.*

I know. It sounds scary, right? Because we spend so much time and energy during pregnancy and afterbirth with people saying things like:

"You'll feel like yourself again soon."

"You'll bounce back."

"You'll get your body back."

"It'll be like you never had a baby."

And while those comments might come with good intentions, they all carry this silent message:

The 'you' before baby is better.

The goal is to return to her.

That your evolution is a problem to fix.

But let me ask you something…would we ever say this to a butterfly?

"Wow, you were way better as a caterpillar."

Nope.

Because change, growth, transformation, it's not just okay, it's powerful.

You'll change. Of course you will. How could you not?

You've literally brought a human into the world. Your body has grown, stretched, birthed and brought life. Your heart has expanded in ways you didn't know were possible.

Your brain is rewiring itself for empathy, protection, and survival. (No really, it's called matrescence and it's the psychological shift into motherhood that's as big as adolescence but no one talks about it.)

You're evolving.

Not disappearing.

You might grieve parts of your *before baby* life. And that's valid.

Maybe you miss your independence, your career focus, your hobbies, your social life, your body the way it used to feel.

That doesn't make you ungrateful.

That makes you human.

This new you?

She's softer in some places. Stronger in others. She's learning to trust her instincts, to set boundaries, to stand up for herself in a way she never did before. She can rock a baby with one hand, answer messages with the other and cry from happiness and exhaustion in the same breath.

She's not less.

She's more.

More depth.

More emotion.

More grit.

More compassion.

More honest about how hard it can all be but how beautiful too.

Reclaiming identity (yes, it's a process).

It might take time to get to know this version of you. That's okay. You're not meant to snap back, emotionally or physically, in six weeks or less. Maybe you do and if you do that is amazing.

Instead of asking, *when will I feel like me again?* maybe ask, *who am I becoming now?*

You get to rebuild.

You get to choose what to carry forward and what to let go.

You get to create a life that works for you, not a Pinterest version of being a woman or a mum.

Let this chapter be your permission to stop striving to go back and start leaning into who you're becoming.

Because this version of you?

She's fierce. She's growing. She's real.

And even if you're not there yet…and you will get there…

I'm proud of her.

WHO WAS I?

This is a tough one!

WHO WAS I BEFORE I BECAME A MOTHER?

Everything from hobbies, what you love to do, favourite foods...

WHAT PARTS OF HER DO I WANT TO BRING INTO THIS NEXT CHAPTER?

Notes

CHAPTER SIX

Your relationship might change; building it back up

When we had our first child, I was 22 and my partner was 23.

Looking back, we were basically babies ourselves. I mean, I didn't even know that mortgage interest was added monthly. I thought you just paid a big chunk and that was it.

I remember feeling too ashamed to ask questions, like not knowing somehow meant I wasn't smart enough to be doing life properly.

The truth?

I hadn't found me yet. My prefrontal cortex wasn't fully developed (that's the bit of your brain that handles decision making and logic, FYI, it doesn't fully settle until you're 25).

Honestly, it wasn't until after COVID, when I was 33, that I really felt like I found my voice. That I stopped being scared of what other people thought and finally felt at home in myself.

So, having a baby at 22? We were unprepared. We loved her, and we were good parents, I know that with every part of me but the adulting part? The managing bills, responsibilities and suddenly being in charge of an actual human life? That was a lot.

We'd gone from a relationship that was carefree, full of parties, sex, fun, freedom…to one that was steeped in responsibility and sleep deprivation. We bickered about money, about who was doing more, who was more tired, etc.

Keeping score is exhausting.

It's so easy to fall into that mindset.

I've been up all night.

You got more sleep.

I've changed ten nappies today.

You've had more of a break, you've not been at work.

Before you know it, you're locked in this invisible competition over who's got it harder.

But there's no winner in that game, only resentment.

What I've learned (and honestly, it took a while) is that it's not about splitting things 50/50, it's about showing up 100/100 in whatever way you can that day.

Because the truth is, you're probably both tired.

You're both navigating new territory. And just because you're doing different things doesn't mean one of you is doing more.

Whether one of you is out working or staying home, whether one of you is breastfeeding or doing night feeds with a bottle, it all counts.

It's all part of the same goal. Raising a tiny human and not totally losing yourselves in the process.

So give each other grace. Appreciate the different roles you both play, even if they look and feel wildly different.

You're a team. And the best teams don't compete against each other, they collaborate.

Let go of the scoreboard.

Then, one day, without fanfare or fireworks, you look across the room or across the dinner table covered in crumbs and you realise, *we made it through.*

You've stopped trying to win or be right, and instead, you start to understand each other in a new way.

You laugh again.

You make each other tea without asking.

You have a moment where your child says something hilarious or your baby finally sleeps through the night, and you look at each other like, *we're actually doing this.*

And somewhere in the chaos, you rediscover your best friend, the one you chose before the nappies and night feeds and 3 a.m. arguments about who's getting up this time.

I want you to think of your upbringing as a house.

Imagine your life so far as being like a house, every brick…laid by your parents, your teachers, your early experiences, your values and you.

When you enter a relationship, most of us unconsciously expect our partner to just move into our house. Because it's familiar. It's what we know. Even if it's got gaps in the walls or a dodgy boiler, it still feels like the *right* way.

But our partners have their own houses.

My husband didn't have a stable upbringing. His house? Held together with whatever he could find, probably built in a storm. And neither of us realised that instead of trying to get the other to move into our house, we needed to build a new house together.

That took time. A lot of it. Like, 10 years.

We actually renovated our physical house in 2021, and it felt symbolic, like we were building something solid, together. Something that reflected us, not who we were told to be or expected to be.

That renovation wasn't just about bricks and paint.

It was healing.

It was grounding.

It was the moment we looked at each other and saw each other, really saw each other for who we were now, not who we used to be.

And we still loved each other during the messy years but we were growing. Separately and together.

And growth is noisy.

It's confusing.

It's uncomfortable.

But it's also beautiful.

So if your relationship feels different, feels off, feels strained… it doesn't mean you've failed. It just means you're being asked to build something new, brick by brick.

Together.

BUILDING SOMETHING NEW...

...Together

IN WHAT WAY HAS OUR RELATIONSHIP CHANGED EMOTIONALLY SINCE BECOMING PARENTS?

NOTES

IN WHAT WAY HAS OUR RELATIONSHIP CHANGED PRACTICALLY SINCE BECOMING PARENTS?

NOTES

How do you feel about these changes?

CHAPTER SEVEN

The quiet loneliness no one warned you about

They said you'd be tired.

They said the baby would cry.

They said your body might feel different.

But no one really said,

You might feel lonely, like ache in your chest, scream into a pillow, invisible kind of lonely.

Not because you don't love your baby.

Not because you're ungrateful.

Not because you're not surrounded by people.

But because this loneliness isn't about being alone.

It's the kind that creeps in when your identity feels blurry, your needs feel invisible and your world has shrunk to four walls, milk feeds and the white noise of a monitor.

It's the kind of loneliness where you can be in a room full of people yet feel like no one really sees you. Where the only adult conversation you've had all day is with the Amazon delivery driver who handed you breast pads with a smile.

It's the type of loneliness that lingers even when your partner comes home, because they don't really get what it's like to be the default parent. The one who knows which cry means hungry and which cry means overtired. The one who's touched out, overstimulated and still somehow...invisible.

Here's what I want you to hear…

This *isn't* weakness. This *isn't* failure. This *is* normal.

Because motherhood, especially in the early days, can be isolating in ways no one prepares you for.

You are not weird for feeling lonely.

You are not failing if this feels hard.

You are not ungrateful if you sometimes wish for a moment to yourself, or a conversation that isn't about nap schedules.

Why does it happen?

Part of this loneliness comes from the shift in identity.

You go from being *you*, maybe a professional, a friend, a partner, a woman with hobbies and opinions to being *mum*. And as beautiful as that role is, it can swallow you whole if you're not careful.

Your brain is also rewiring itself during matrescence (yes, that's a thing, a whole developmental phase for becoming a mother). You're becoming someone new.

And with every change, there's loss. Even when the change is good.

And don't get me started on society. We live in a world that encourages independence, hustle culture and *bouncing back*.

But motherhood? It requires that village we talked about earlier. It demands slowness. It thrives on connection. And when that's missing, it's no wonder we feel so alone.

As a person, I've always been more introvert than extrovert. Give me a quiet afternoon with my cats and a cup of tea over small talk and socialising any day. But even with two school-age children and a newborn, I felt it, that unmistakable pang of loneliness.

The kind no one warns you about.

It wasn't loud. It didn't scream for attention. It just crept in slowly, making the days feel longer and the silence feel heavier. Then one day, on the ever chaotic school WhatsApp group, a message popped up:

Does anyone fancy a coffee this Friday?

Now, I normally wouldn't bite. Not my scene. I'd usually scroll past and stay in my comfort zone (home). But something inside me whispered, *just go*.

These were mums I barely knew. Our kids had just started nursery together. We were still in that awkward, *which one's yours?* phase. But I went.

And you know what? Only two of us showed up.

Best thing that ever happened.

That one coffee morning became every Friday.

Unlimited cups, little ones running wild, and two tired mums who talked and laughed and ranted and healed bit by bit.

No judgment.

No pretending.

Just real talk over one of my favourite things, caffeine.

I don't know what made me go that day, maybe the universe nudged me. But what I found was more than just company. I found a safe place, a fellow warrior, a lifeline.

She's still that for me. And I'll always be thankful.

So if you're feeling that familiar ache of loneliness, I want to tell you something:

You don't have to be a social butterfly.

You don't need to fake a smile or force conversation.

You just need to say yes, just once, and let that small brave moment open the door.

To her, thank you.

You saved me in the loneliness.

Go find that friend…she is out there looking for you too!

THIS PART CAN FEEL HARD...

Take your time and let it all out!

HOW HAVE I BEEN FEELING LATELY ABOUT CONNECTING WITH PEOPLE AND FRIENDSHIPS?

What emotions surface when you think about the people around you?

NEGATIVE V POSITIVE

What emotions do you feel when thinking about doing something new?

What positive things can come out of starting or trying something new?

What's stopping you from reaching out or saying yes to something social right now?

CHAPTER EIGHT

It's OK not to love every moment (no gold star for martyrdom)

Sometimes I didn't enjoy it.

You're allowed to not enjoy parts of motherhood.

You're allowed to want to scream into a pillow when your toddler throws a full-body tantrum at 8:15am while you're holding packed lunches, two water bottles and a half-dressed baby.

You're allowed to feel frustrated, burnt out, touched out and completely done.

That doesn't make you a bad mum. That makes you human.

I remember the school run phase that nearly broke me. One child was an angel, smiling, skipping along, ready to go. The other? A full-blown chaos goblin. Screaming, lying on the pavement, absolutely feral because their sock 'felt weird'. Every other mum seemed calm, hair brushed, with matching lunchboxes and perfectly plaited hair with bows! Meanwhile, I was one shoe in, one slipper out the door, wondering what the hell I'd done wrong in a past life.

The worst part wasn't the tantrum. It was the shame. The glares. The whispered, *just ignore him* or the classic *he needs boundaries*. The inner voice that said, *why can't you control this? why are you failing?* I was listening to it all but none of it seemed to apply to my real life.

And deep down, I was quietly hating this phase.

Yes, I said it. There were moments I hated it. I resented my husband for leaving the house, for having adult conversations.

I was drowning in tiny humans and everywhere was telling me I should feel grateful.

I *was* grateful but I was also exhausted, bored with the monotony and desperate for five bloody minutes.

And let's not forget the guilt. Gremlin Mum Guilt showed up constantly. When I looked at going back to some sort of work it barely even covered the childcare costs. I felt trapped.

Here is the thing.

Loving your children and hating parts of motherhood *can* exist in the same breath.

You don't need to earn some invisible gold star for powering through with a smile. You need support. You need space.

You need to be real.

So if you're in the thick of it, if you're looking around wondering why everyone else seems so *together* just know this: behind every calm-looking school mum is a woman who has definitely (possibly) also cried into a cereal box at 7am one time or another.

You're not alone.

Sit with the hard stuff.

Honour how you feel.

You're doing the hardest job in the world, and it's OK to say,

"Today, this is really, really hard."

You can love your children with all your heart and soul. Finding days hard or hating phases doesn't mean you don't love them with everything you have.

NO GOLD STAR FOR MARTYRDOM

If you want a gold star here it is.

From me to you!

WHAT ARE THE MOMENTS I HAVE BEEN FINDING ESPECIALLY HARD LATELY?

I've started you off on the next page.

NOW REFRAME IT

I am struggling, I feel like I am doing everything and it's making me miserable.	I am not communicating my feelings very well, I need to have an open and honest conversation when I feel I need support.

THOUGHTS

Try to write things you think you shouldn't be thinking.

Be honest with yourself, this is your space.

CHAPTER NINE

Every version of birth comes with its own path

Prepare for recovery, not just labour.

Everyone's asked you if *you're ready for the baby...*

You've packed the hospital bag. You've practised your breathing, read the birth plan (okay, maybe rewritten it three times).

But there's something no one talks about enough.

Birth is a moment in time.

Recovery is a process.

And it deserves just as much attention, if not more.

Because while labour might be intense, it's usually over in a matter of hours (okay, sometimes a lot of hours). But recovery? That's the real marathon. That's the bit where your body is trying to heal, your hormones are changing like a 90s mood ring, and you're caring for a tiny human while running on broken sleep and cold tea.

No one prepares you for:

- The postpartum bleeding (yes, why does no one tell you it's not a dainty trickle?).
- Stitches (or just soreness that makes sitting feel like a full contact sport).
- Leaking boobs, cracked nipples and *is this normal?!* questions every five minutes.

- The emotional rollercoaster, crying because you're happy, then crying because you can't find your hairbrush.
- How LONG recovery actually takes (hint: it's not 6 weeks and done).

Yet most antenatal classes barely mention it. You're left thinking that the real challenge is getting the baby out, when really, the big work begins after.

Recovery isn't just about your body, it's about your whole self.

And it's not linear.

Some days you'll feel strong and powerful.

Others you'll feel like you've been hit by a bus and then reversed over by your breast pump.

And that's whether you've had a vaginal birth or a c-section, because every version of birth comes with its own recovery path.

Here's what recovery really looks like:

- Rest. Real rest. Not, *sleep when the baby sleeps* (because we all know that's a joke) but giving yourself permission to slow down.
- Nourishment. Feeding yourself. Hydrating. Letting people cook for you without guilt.
- Support. Whether that's your partner, your mum, your best friend or a WhatsApp group at 2am. Recovery isn't meant to be done on your own.
- Movement, but the gentle kind. Think pelvic floor, breath work, core connection. Not bootcamp.
- Emotional space. To cry, to journal, to process. To not have it all together.

If you're yet to have your baby, instead of just packing the birth bag, try these tips:

- Pack comfy pants (the big ones, the Bridget Jones specials).
- Stock up on pads (yes, even if you're having a c-section).
- Prep some easy to digest meals or freezer stash if you can.
- Learn about your pelvic floor now, not when it's shouting at you.
- Have a plan for rest and help post birth. Meals. Visitors to have baby cuddles while you shower.

You didn't just birth a baby, you birthed a whole new you.

You are healing physically, emotionally, spiritually.

That deserves attention.

Kindness.

Recovery is hard and every person recovers at a different rate.

You're not *behind*. It literally takes months.

Stop looking at Instagram posts of influencers who have *bounced* back.

You're human. And you're doing one of the most incredible things on the planet, bringing life into the world.

So prepare for it. Honour it. And don't forget, you're worth looking after too.

WHAT DOES MY BODY NEED MOST RIGHT NOW?

Be honest with yourself. Judgement free pages here!

WHAT ARE MY BIGGEST FEARS OR UNKNOWNS ABOUT RECOVERY?

You've grown and birthed a human, you're pretty awesome!

WHAT DOES REST ACTUALLY LOOK LIKE FOR ME?

HOW CAN I CREATE MORE OF IT?

If you could give yourself one message of compassion for today, what would it be?

CHAPTER TEN

What the hell is a pelvic floor and why should I care?

She is a Diva!

Let's just start by saying: if the words 'pelvic floor' sound like something that belongs in a Victorian plumbing manual, you are not alone.

Before babies, chances are you never gave it a second thought.

Now?

You might sneeze and do a little prayer.

Or laugh and cross your legs.

Or do a star jump and suddenly remember you were once warned about this mythical muscle group a long time ago.

So let's break it down, woman to woman, because your pelvic floor deserves some attention. And you know what? Let's stop just calling it 'the pelvic floor'. Let's call her Diva. Because she's holding up the entire club, and frankly, she deserves more respect than she's getting.

She's not the sexiest of muscles, she's not glamorous, but she is powerful. And girl, you're going to want her working *for* you, not *against* you.

Here comes some science for you, I will keep it short and to the point. Think of her like a hammock of muscles that sits at the base of your pelvis. She holds up your bladder, bowel and uterus (thanks for showing up team).

She is involved in peeing, pooing, sex, birth and yep, pretty much everything that makes us human and a little bit chaotic.

During pregnancy, Diva is under major pressure. And childbirth, especially vaginal delivery, can stretch, strain or injure her. Even c-sections aren't a total pass, because carrying a baby still adds to her load.

We get taught how to think about our birth, time contractions and pack a hospital bag with more snacks than sense. But no one sits us down and says, *Hey, one day you might be pushing a buggy while clenching for dear life, and that's not normal, it's a sign you need to start giving your Diva some love.*

Because society's weird about women's bodies.

Especially when it comes to leaking, healing and pleasure.

You've seen the ads, those ones with women doing star jumps in crisp white leggings like leaking is just a fun little side effect of being a mum.

No thank you.

Yes, absorbent pads have their place, sometimes they're a short term safety net while you heal or seek support but they should never be the solution.

Masking the issue isn't fixing it.

And leaking? It might be common but it is not your new normal.

You deserve better.

You deserve to feel good in your body again.

You deserve to jump, sneeze, orgasm and run without fear.

You deserve to know your body and how to take care of it.

Signs your Diva might need some love:

- Leaking when you sneeze, cough, laugh or exercise.
- A feeling of heaviness or pressure *down there.*
- Pain during sex.
- Struggling to hold in wind or get to the toilet in time.
- Just feeling… like something's not quite right.

These things are common but they are not normal. And help is out there. A women's health physio can be life changing, they exist and they're amazing.

So what can you do?

Start with awareness. Just knowing this matters. You're already ahead of where most of us were.

- Pelvic floor exercises. But done right, not just squeezing randomly at traffic lights.
- Breathe well. Deep breathing supports your pelvic floor, tension messes with it.
- See a specialist. A postnatal check with a women's health physio should be the norm, not a luxury.

If you're reading this thinking, *crap, this is me*, breathe.

You are not broken.

You are not weak.

You are not less than before because your body is still recovering from growing and birthing a whole human being (even if it was years ago)!

This can all be healed.

Just like a bicep curl builds arm strength, consistent, kind attention builds pelvic floor Diva power.

Because she is an incredible, resilient, wise muscle.

She just needs your support, not your silence.

JUST ME AND MY DIVA!

Use the next pages as a daily pelvic floor check-in and simple guide. You just need 5 minutes a day!

Take a moment before you grab your phone or race into the chaos.

Either sitting on the edge of the bed or standing while brushing your teeth:

Close your eyes.

Take three slow, deep breaths into your abdominals.

Ask yourself:

- How does my body feel today?
- Do I feel tension or pressure 'down there'?
- Did I leak yesterday or feel weak during movement?

This is about listening to your body... Diva doesn't like to be ignored.

This is your daily strength building moment. Think of it like Diva Training!

3-Part Connection:

Breathe in and allow your abdominals and pelvic floor to gently relax.

Breathe out and gently lift and squeeze your pelvic floor muscles (as if stopping wee or holding in wind), then release fully.

Repeat. Do this 10 times, slow and controlled.

Pro Tip - Count "lift 1-2-3, release 1-2-3."

Just you, your breath and your body!

How does your body feel today?
Do you feel tension or pressure 'down there'?
This isn't about judgement, this is about tuning in.

CHAPTER ELEVEN

Your body might feel like a stranger, but she's still yours

The mirror moment.

Let's talk about the moment you look in the mirror after having a baby and think…*whose body is this?*

The skin feels so weird, stomach soft and empty, your boobs are sore or leaking or suddenly alien. Your scar might be tender, your hips wider, your hair falling out in clumps, your ribs…who knew your rib cage moved?

You feel like a guest in your own skin.

A version of yourself you didn't sign up for.

And yet this body? She carried life. She expanded, stretched, broke open and still stood up the next day. She may not look exactly like you anymore.

But she *is* you.

Even when she feels unfamiliar.

Even when you're mourning what was.

Even when you scroll and compare and question.

Bouncing back I hate that phrase with a passion!

You're not a trampoline.

This isn't about *getting your body back*. Your body never left!

Because you never lost her, she's been right here the whole time, doing impossible things quietly.

It's okay to grieve the body you had. That body might have felt strong, sexy, controlled. Maybe she danced, maybe she ran marathons, maybe she fit into your favourite jeans. You're allowed to miss her.

But don't miss the chance to meet the version of you now.

The one who knows more, feels deeper and has endured more than she ever thought possible.

You are not *just* a vessel.

Your body didn't *just* carry your baby.

She carried you too, through anxiety, anticipation, pain and joy.

She doesn't deserve punishment. She deserves patience.

She deserves kindness, movement that feels good, rest when it's needed and clothes that fit her, not the old version of you.

This chapter of your life is not about erasing the marks of motherhood. It's about reclaiming your body as something more than a baby making machine.

She is still yours.

She's evolving.

She's wise.

She is worth celebrating.

Let's rethink beauty…

Stretch marks? They're lightning bolts of growth.

A soft belly? It's a cushion that held your child.

Scars? They're not flaws they are stitches in your story.

Your body is not ruined. It's reborn.

If you're struggling with being in your own skin try these daily mantras:

My body is different, but she is still strong.

I can miss the old me, and still love the new one.

I deserve to feel at home in my skin again.

Real women, real bodies, real stories.

As someone who has worked in fitness for my whole adult life, I've worked with women from all walks of life, mums, students, professionals, grandmothers, newly postpartum and those decades into motherhood.

Every single one of them, no matter their size, strength or fitness level, had something unbelievably cruel to say about their body at some point.

It's almost like a ritual. Sometimes it's the first thing that comes out of their mouths and other times it takes a few sessions but eventually it comes out:

"Sorry I'm such a mess."

"Ugh, don't look at my stomach. It's disgusting."

"Once I lose this belly, I'll finally feel okay."

"I've had three kids, so this is just what happens, right?"

"I hate how my thighs rub together when I run."

"Have you seen my knees they're flabby."

And here's the thing, I never once saw what they were seeing.

I saw resilience. Power. Grit. A woman juggling work and family and a million invisible things and still showing up for herself.

But when I looked in their eyes, I saw disgust and shame.

Deep, unfair shame.

Not because of their bodies but because of what they'd been taught to believe about them.

I once trained a mum of four who could lift amazingly; she was so strong. But all she could say was, "I just want to fit into my pre baby jeans. I feel like a failure every time I can't button them up".

I trained a woman in her fifties who told me she didn't want to wear shorts even in summer because of her knees. Her knees. "They're just too saggy," she said. She could do push ups better than most twenty year olds, but she couldn't see past her skin.

Another mum burst into tears mid-session after a plank hold, not because it was hard, but because she said, "I used to be so fit. Now I feel like a blob".

This same woman had literally birthed twins the year before.

But that wasn't enough for her to feel proud of her body.

What they said vs what I saw:

We've been taught to shrink ourselves.

Not just physically but emotionally, too. To apologise for taking up space.

To explain why we haven't *bounced back*.

To feel *less than* because our bodies are more lived in.

And you know what? It's exhausting. And it's everywhere.

Society has been quietly (and sometimes loudly) telling us from the beginning: *be smaller, be quieter, be more agreeable, be easier to look at.*

From the moment we were called *cute* or *pretty* instead of being called *smart* or *strong*, the message was there. From corsets to the heroin chic 90s, to the filtered perfection of today's social feeds, women's bodies have always been a battleground, scrutinised, controlled and commodified.

We see it in headlines shaming celebrities post baby bodies. We hear it in the comments that seem harmless but cut deep: "You've lost weight, you look amazing!" as if that's the highest praise a woman can receive.

We've been taught to shrink ourselves.

We feel it when we avoid photos, when we stare at ourselves sideways in the mirror, when we suck in our bellies out of habit.

And the worst part? We've absorbed it. It's in the way we speak to ourselves and sometimes, in the way we speak to each other.

So let's stop.

Let's call bullshit on all of it.

Because you do not need to *fix* your body in order to be worthy.

You are a powerhouse of life and love and effort.

Your body tells a story and it's not a horror one, by the way.

It's epic.

One with stretch marks and softness and strength. With tired feet and milk stained bras. With moments of dancing in the kitchen and crying on the bathroom floor. With all the magic and mess that comes with raising humans while trying to remember who you are.

And we need to stop commenting on other women's bodies altogether. Not because we're being overly sensitive but because it's just not our business. Whether she's bigger, smaller, taller, shorter, newly postpartum or ten years in, we lift each other up.

Period.

Because if one of us is still at war with herself, none of us are free.

This is the sisterhood.

The rebellion.

The quiet revolution of saying: *I like me, as I am*.

And I honour you, as you are, too.

MY BODY IS STILL MINE AND SHE IS BEAUTIFUL!

Give it a go... try saying it out loud! Repeat it over and over.
Your body has created, carried and birthed life!

WHAT DO OTHER PEOPLE THINK OF ME?

Write on the outside of the heart what you think other people think of your body and appearance.

Write on the inside of the heart what you think other people think of you as a person.

WHAT DO OTHER PEOPLE ACTUALLY THINK OF ME?

Ask other people and write on the outside of the heart what they think of your body and appearance.

Ask other people and write on the inside what they think of you as a person.

How do you feel about what people said?
Did it change your opinion of yourself?

CHAPTER TWELVE

Sex after baby, what they don't put in the leaflet

Yes, we are going there...so if you're prudish, don't skip this chapter, read it anyway.

There are about a million leaflets handed to you during pregnancy.

Ones about feeding, bathing, sleep, poo (so much about poo, poo colours, poo types), but barely anything about sex. And if it is mentioned, it's usually just a dry, clinical, '*you can resume intercourse when the bleeding stops or around 6 weeks postpartum.'*

Cool. But it felt like my uterus nearly fell out. I'm wearing a pad the size of a mattress, and you want me to what now?

Hear this loud and clear. There is no magic switch at six weeks that makes you ready for sex again.

There is no *normal* timeline.

There is only *your* body, *your* mind, *your* readiness.

This is the physical part, it's not gross (mostly) but it will help you understand some of what your body is feeling or going through.

Your hormones are all over the place. Oestrogen drops, which means your natural lubrication may have left the building. Lube is not optional; it's possibly your new bestie.

You might feel dry, tender, tight, swollen or just not right.

That's okay.

If you had stitches, a tear or a c-section, there can be numbness or nerve sensitivity.

You might even feel like your vagina is a different shape. (Because for a while, it is.)

And just so we're all on the same page, painful sex is not something you should *just put up with*. That's a sign your body needs support, not suffering.

When 6 weeks means nothing:

I remember hearing '*six weeks*' thrown around like it was some magic number. As if on that day, a switch would flick and I'd be ready, body, mind and libido like nothing had ever changed.

After my first baby (a c-section), if someone had come to me and said, "You never have to have sex again," honestly, I might have taken them up on it. It's not that I didn't love my partner. It's not that I didn't appreciate intimacy. But I just…didn't feel like *me* anymore.

My body felt weird. Squishy. Foreign. I didn't feel sexy, I barely felt functional. And more than that, I felt guilty.

Like somehow, by not wanting sex, I wasn't being a *good* partner. Like I was broken. Selfish, even.

But here's the wild thing, none of that guilt came from my partner. He didn't pressure me. He didn't expect anything.

Those thoughts?

All self-inflicted. And isn't that just awful what we say internally to ourselves?

We internalise these silent expectations, like we're meant to bounce back, be grateful, be available, be everything to everyone. No one tells us that sex after birth can feel … complicated. Tender. Scary. Awkward. And that it's all okay.

What helped? Time. And honest conversations, when I finally allowed them.

Connecting with my partner in other ways. Learning to use my voice, instead of staying quiet in my shame.

I wish someone had told me back then:

You don't owe anyone your body, especially not before you're ready.

Desire will come back, on *your* terms, not on a schedule.

If you're reading this, you can start now. Your body is yours. Your timeline is valid. And you don't need to rush something your heart (or vagina) isn't ready for.

Your brain is still quite possibly in survival mode. You might have been touched all day, boobs grabbed by a baby, body leaned on, arms constantly holding.

So the last thing you want is more touching. That's not a broken libido. That's sensory overload.

You might also feel:

- Disconnected from your body, especially if it still feels like it belongs to your baby more than you.
- Worried about how it will feel or how you look.
- Resentful, especially if your partner didn't go through the same physical rollercoaster.

It's not just about when you're ready, but how you redefine intimacy.

The first time post baby can feel like losing your virginity all over again but with added fear, tension and maybe a baby monitor crackling in the background.

Here's the golden rule: start where you are.

- That might mean just any type of contact.
- That might mean snogging like teenagers on the sofa.
- That might mean talking openly about what you need emotionally and physically before anything even starts.

If you're in a relationship, this is for them too.

Here's the memo: Go slow. Ask questions. Be gentle. Take *'not tonight'* like a champ.

This isn't about rejection, it's about rebuilding.

If you're not in a relationship, that doesn't mean intimacy is off the table. This includes you too. Reconnecting with yourself, feeling desirable again for you, matters just as much.

You are still sensual, still worthy, still allowed to explore pleasure.

You're not less than for not wanting sex. You're also not broken for wanting it sooner than '*expected'*. Go with your feelings. Let them guide you, there is no right or wrong if it is you making the decision.

You're not selfish for prioritising your own comfort.

And there's no shame in saying, "I'm not there yet." Or, "I want to try, but I need support."

This chapter isn't about giving you a deadline, it's about giving you permission. To take your time. To ask for what you need. To rediscover your body on your terms.

Because guess what?

You are still sexy. Still powerful. Still worthy of pleasure.

Even in those nappy pants. Especially in those nappy pants.

Take a quiet moment. Breathe deep. Get comfy.

Now, use the next page to answer these questions honestly, gently and without judgement.

WHAT DOES INTIMACY MEAN TO ME RIGHT NOW?

It might not be about sex. It might be about touch, safety, laughter, deep conversation.

HOW DO I FEEL IN MY BODY LATELY?

Not how you 'should' feel. How you really feel.

Safe? Disconnected? Curious? Tired? Strong?

WHAT DO I NEED IN ORDER TO FEEL READY OR EVEN JUST CURIOUS ABOUT INTIMACY AGAIN?

More rest? Communication? Space? Help with the baby? A date night?

MY FEELINGS AROUND INTIMACY

What emotions do you feel around sex? Let them out. Fear, confusion, shame, pressure, excitement. Let it out. These are valid

What would perfect intimacy look like for you now?

What are the thoughts you carry about sex since having a baby?

What beliefs about sex or your body do you want to let go of?

CHAPTER THIRTEEN

Fitness v flat stomach (strength and sanity)

Fitness after birth.

Now, I'm not saying don't move your body or that you shouldn't care how you feel physically. But fitness after birth? It should be about strength, healing and your sanity. I've trained a lot of women over the years.

“I just want my old jeans to fit again.”

“I hate looking in the mirror.”

“Why does my tummy still look pregnant?”

“I feel weak carrying the car seat and the baby.”

Ever heard those words come out of your mouth?

Let's start where you are. Let's move to feel strong. Let's reconnect you to you.

It's not about *burning off* the baby weight.

It's not about chasing some bikini body fantasy that was photoshopped into your head by Instagram.

It's about regaining confidence in how your body moves, how it carries you, how it helps you show up each day for your baby, yes, but most importantly, for yourself.

A flat stomach doesn't mean fitness.

Some of the fittest, strongest women I've trained had soft bellies, stretch marks and cores that needed rebuilding from the inside out. That's where we start, your deep core, your pelvic floor Diva, your breath, your posture, your alignment.

You don't need to bounce. You don't need to sweat buckets and feel broken. You need movement that builds you up, not breaks you down.

Movement that says. I deserve this time. I deserve to feel strong. I deserve to feel good in my skin again.

There's no before and after picture here.

There's just you now.

Because you are not an '*after*'. You're a whole damn work of art in progress. You deserve workouts that honour that. Whether that's walking with the buggy, postnatal Pilates, strength training or dancing around the kitchen with your baby in a sling.

Movement is medicine.

You are allowed to move for your mind, not your jeans size.

You can be soft and strong at the same time.

Your body isn't a problem to fix. It's a partner to celebrate.

So ditch the tummy-taming narrative. Choose fitness for you not for the mirror, not for Instagram, not for approval.

For your strength. For your sanity. For the woman inside you who still deserves to feel alive.

And to the women who love to train…this is for you too.

To the ones who miss the burn, the sweat, the ache of muscles that say, *hell yes, I showed up for myself today.*

To the ones who feel like movement is their reset button, their release valve. I see you. And I get it.

You don't need to apologise for wanting to feel like an athlete again.

You don't have to tone down your fire because you're a mum now.

But here's what I'll gently remind you.

It's not about *getting you back*.

It's about rebuilding forward with respect, with patience and with your powerhouse body that's done more than most will ever understand.

You're not weak for modifying.

You're not failing if you're slower, heavier or breathless.

Your strength didn't leave you, it just changed shape.

And when you train? Do it because it makes you feel like you again. Not because you need to prove anything to anyone.

If you've had a c-section, your body has been through major abdominal surgery and it deserves time, patience and so much kindness. You might feel a disconnect from your core, numbness or tenderness around your scar. That's normal, but it's also a sign to take things slowly. Start with gentle breath work, scar massage (when healed) and core reconnection exercises, not crunches or planks right away.

Likewise, if you suspect or know you have diastasis recti (the separation of the abdominal muscles), don't panic. Healing doesn't mean doing *more* it means doing the right kind of movement that brings those muscles back into alignment and support. A women's health physio can guide you here; their advice is gold.

GOING AT MY OWN PACE!

Try our weekly planner as a start... go at your own pace!

Monday – Core & Connection (10 mins)

Gentle deep core & pelvic floor activation.

· Diaphragmatic breathing.

· Try lying on your back, knees bent, one hand on your abdomen, one on your chest. Slow breaths, gentle pelvic floor lifts.

Think, reconnect, don't 'suck in'.

Tuesday – Walk & Listen (20-30 mins)

· Pram walk, baby carrier stroll or solo if you can steal it.
· Plug in a feel good podcast or just breathe.
· New to movement? If this is the only movement you do this week, that's enough.
· More experienced? Add light hills or increase pace slightly.

Fresh air can heal the soul!

Wednesday – Rest and Stretch (5–10 mins)

· Hamstrings, chest, hips and all those places that ache post baby.
· Foam roller if you have it.
· Add gentle mobility, cat, cows, hip circles, shoulder rolls.

Think of this as your body's 'thank you' day.

Thursday – Low Impact Strength (15-20 mins)

· Bodyweight squats.
· Wall push ups or incline push ups.
· Glute bridges.
· Resistance band rows (if you've got one).
· No weights needed, just focus on form and slow, controlled movement.

I AM MOVING FOR MY BODY AND MY MIND

Friday - Dance or Flow (10-15 mins)

· Put on a playlist and move like nobody's watching (because probably no one is) Or try a 10 min postnatal yoga session.

Movement can be fun, silly, sexy, messy, let it feel like YOU!

Saturday – 'Me' Move (Your Choice)

· What feels good today? Maybe nothing? Maybe a swim?
· Maybe chasing your toddler counts (because let's be honest, it does).
· This is your 'no rules' day.

Sunday – Rest & Reflect

· Full rest day or some light stretching with baby on the mat.

How did moving make you feel this week?
Celebrate your wins, even if it's,
I showed up once. That's huge!

CHAPTER FOURTEEN

What is diastasis recti? (and how do I know if I have it?)

Diastasis recti is the natural separation of the abdominal muscles during pregnancy to make space for your growing baby. For some women, this gap doesn't close fully on its own after birth and it can affect core strength, stability and even posture. It's super common and super fixable with the right approach.

It is one of the top reasons women who come to me struggle with regaining core connection.

You can have a look yourself to see if you have a Diastasis Recti:

- A visible 'doming' or bulge down the middle of your belly when you sit up or strain.
- A soft gap between your abdominal muscles, often around the belly button.
- A feeling of weakness or lack of support through your core.
- Lower back pain or a feeling like your insides aren't quite 'held together'.

You can gently check yourself lying down with knees bent, using your fingers to feel the space between the muscles, but for peace of mind and proper support, see a women's health physio if you're unsure. You deserve expert eyes on your recovery.

MY CORE IS MORE THAN AESTHETICS, IT IS MY STRENGTH!

Try our simple starter core routine.

These movements are designed to gently rebuild your deep core (transverse abdominals and pelvic floor) not just your 'six pack'.

Do these daily or every other day, at your own pace. No equipment needed.

Always check in with your breath.

Diaphragmatic Breathing (2-3 minutes)

Lie on your back or sit tall. Inhale slowly, allowing your ribs to expand. Exhale slowly through pursed lips, feeling your core gently draw inward.

This helps re-engage the deep core system.

Pelvic Floor and Core Connection (10 reps)

On your next exhale, gently lift your pelvic floor (imagine stopping wind or wee) and draw your lower tummy in like zipping up a pair of jeans. Hold while you still keep breathing, then release fully.

Heel Slides (10 reps per leg)

Lie on your back, knees bent. Slide one heel away from your body as you exhale and engage your deep core. Inhale to return.
Keep your back neutral and ribs soft.

Shoulder Bridges (10 reps)

Great for core and hip strength. Press through your heels to lift your hips while keeping ribs drawn down. Exhale as you lift, inhale as you lower. Engage your pelvic floor gently at the top.

Try to imagine peeling your spine off the floor.

Side-Lying Clamshells (10 per side)

Lie on your side, knees bent, feet together. Lift your top knee while keeping feet together. Great for glutes (your powerhouse muscles) which support your core and back.

A Gentle Reminder.

This isn't about getting 'flat' it's about getting strong. It's about function. It's about feeling like you again, steady, centred, capable.

Want to follow along to a video? There is a QR code at the end of the book with lots of freebee courses for you to enjoy!

How does your body feel?

What would help you feel connected?

CHAPTER FIFTEEN

The internet doesn't know your baby

No…she knows a lot…because *obviously* Google, Siri, ChatGPT, Gemini are all female, but she does not know your baby!

Google knows a lot of things. Like the circumference of the moon, how to make sourdough, or what to do when your toddler shoves a popcorn kernel up their nose (yep totally happened to us).

But one thing Google (and forums, Facebook groups and that influencer with the perfect neutral nursery) does not know?

Your baby.

Not their temperament. Not their feeding cues. Not their sleep patterns or their little quirks or what calms them at 3am. The internet doesn't know your baby, and it certainly doesn't know you as a mother.

But it can feel like it does, can't it?

You find yourself up at 2:14am, scrolling on your phone in the blue light darkness, looking for answers:

Is it normal if my baby only naps for 23 minutes?

Should I be feeding every two hours still?

When will I feel like myself again?

And suddenly, your screen is a portal to thousands of other people's babies all sleeping better, feeding more efficiently, meeting milestones earlier.

Their mums? Calm. Confident. Minimalist wardrobes. Apparently, no leaking boobs or tears in supermarket aisles.

You close your phone feeling like you're doing everything wrong.

But here's what I want you to remember:

They're not raising *your* baby.

Their routines, their methods, their miracle swaddles, those might work for them.

That doesn't mean they'll work for you. And it definitely doesn't mean you're failing if they don't.

Your baby is a whole human being, not a checklist in a parenting manual or an algorithm in a sleep app. They are allowed to be different. They are allowed to need you in ways the internet didn't predict.

You are not a project manager. You're a mum.

This isn't productivity. This is a relationship.

I remember once Googling, *how long should my 5 week old sleep at night?* and landing in a terrifying wormhole of baby sleep training advice that made me feel like I'd already ruined everything because I wasn't doing a routine. I cried. My baby cried. My partner hid the phone.

What I needed wasn't another online chart.

I needed someone to say, "You know your baby. Trust yourself. And you're doing just fine."

So let me say it to you now.

You know your baby. Trust yourself. And you're doing just fine.

Some gentle reminders:

The internet is a tool, not a bible. Use it if it helps. Shut it down if it doesn't.

You can try something that worked for someone else and still decide it's not for you.

There is no *one size fits all* in parenting. Because your baby isn't just any baby. They're *your* baby.

Real babies are messy and unpredictable. So are real mums. And that's more than OK, it's normal.

Use social media for fun and entertainment (I am not a social media hater!) remove accounts that make you feel bad, keep the cat videos, keep the stuff that makes you smile and chuckle at a 3am feed.

I LOVE TO SCROLL I HATE TO SCROLL

Reflection and time for you!

WHAT DO I DO MOST ONLINE?

Not sure? Check your phone usage... it can be an eye opener!

HOW DO I FEEL AFTER BEING ONLINE?

Does it feel a positive or negative experience? How do I feel when I move away from it?

MAKE ONLINE POSITIVE

Write in here all the things online you enjoy

Write in here all the things online that make you feel negative

What does your brain need? Screen limits?
Removing apps? Or do you love it all?

CHAPTER SIXTEEN

No one sleeps (and it's not your fault)

If you're reading this with one eye open, holding a lukewarm tea in one hand and a baby who refuses to be put down in the other, welcome.

You're officially part of the, *I haven't slept in what feels like years,* club. There's no badge but there should be.

You might have tried everything. The books. The apps. The white noise. That oddly intense Instagram sleep consultant. Maybe even whispered "drowsy but awake" like a sleep spell while slowly backing out of the room, only for your baby to spring up like a jack in the box the second your hand left their little body.

You are not alone.

Newborns aren't biologically designed to sleep through the night.

They wake up a lot. That's actually how they survive. Tiny tummies, primal instincts and a deep biological need to check in on their favourite human (hi, that's you).

But somehow, we still end up thinking we've done something wrong when our babies don't magically sleep in neat three hour chunks.

Not your energy. Not your bedtime routine. Not the fact that you let them nap on your chest while watching Netflix.

Some things that I deeply believe, and it's your choice if you believe them too, but you are not spoiling your baby by holding them.

Nope. You can't spoil a baby with love.

There is no magic time or age when they should be sleeping through the night. Who is putting this out there? The parenting police? Every baby is different.

If you're showing up, loving, comforting and keeping that tiny human alive, you're doing it more than right.

What works for others doesn't always work for you but let me tell you what worked for me:

- Safe co-sleeping (lifesaver for me, look it up if you haven't).
- Embracing contact naps. You are the cot now (do it safely).
- Letting go of rigid *rules*. Sleep isn't linear.
- Resting when they nap, even if it's sitting in silence with your eyes closed.
- Asking for help. And doing it without guilt.

And if nothing works today? That's okay too. Some days, survival is the goal. And honestly? That's enough.

It is ok to resent the people who tell you their baby sleeps through. That is bloody great for them. Give them your best high five. But it is nothing you're doing wrong or not doing.

Some babies sleep long periods and some don't sleep much at all.

'*Will I ever sleep again*?' was a constant in my head.

Yes. Yes you will! At some point, this phase will feel like a distant memory and you'll be trying to get them OUT of bed.

Sleep is really not a reflection of how *good* a parent you are.

It's just one part of a messy, beautiful, chaotic picture.

And you? You're already doing it.

SLEEP.

Sleep is not a reflection of how 'good' a parent you are.

If you feel so inclined...pop this on your fridge, your breast pad box or your formula.

Sleep will come. Your baby will grow. And you will feel like yourself again. But for now, if all you did today was love them, you did everything right.

WHAT HELPS ME COPE WITH LESS SLEEP?

How are you feeling about sleep and your baby sleeping?

Are you desperate for a routine or are you rolling with it?

WRITE IT ALL OUT

CHAPTER SEVENTEEN

Babies cry

You might be pacing the kitchen, *shushing* like a broken sprinkler system, wondering if it's colic or wind or the wrong brand of wipes or that you ate dairy last night.

You might feel like your baby is the only one who seems to be screaming while everyone else's are apparently meditating peacefully.

Crying is how babies communicate. It doesn't mean you're failing. It doesn't mean they're broken. It doesn't mean you are.

Yes, it's biologically designed to grab your attention (and spike your cortisol), because you're their person. But crying isn't always a cue that something is wrong; it's also how babies process this big, noisy, bright new world.

It's how they discharge tension, how they settle their nervous systems and sometimes, it's just what they need to do.

And yes, it is really hard to hear. Especially when you've done all the things. Changed, fed, burped, cuddled, rocked, swayed. And still…the crying.

You're allowed to feel frustrated. You're allowed to want to hide in the bathroom for a moment just to breathe. You're allowed to hand your baby to your partner and walk away for five minutes with earplugs in and a cup of tea (even if it's gone cold again).

That doesn't make you a bad mum. That makes you a human mum.

There is deep strength in recognising your limits and caring for yourself so you can keep showing up. Because you are showing up. Even when it feels like nothing's working.

My sister had her children a little later than I did. By the time her first baby arrived, I was already eight months into life with my third. So I'd been in the thick of it and out the other side, a few times before.

She took to motherhood like an absolute pro, taking it all in her stride. But when her second came along two years later…that's when things got real.

I remember the messages in our family WhatsApp group. Around 6 p.m., every day like clockwork, the dread would set in.

She'd write, "It's starting…" like she was bracing for battle. The evenings were the hardest, what so many call the '*witching hour*'.

Her baby would cry and cry and nothing helped. My mum would head over most evenings to help because juggling a toddler and a screaming newborn is a test even superheroes would struggle with.

We all pitched in. My mum would rock her, my dad would take her on walks around the street. But nothing seemed to settle her. And not because anyone was doing anything wrong, but simply because some babies just cry.

Sometimes for no clear reason. Sometimes because they're overtired, or overstimulated, or just figuring out how to be in this noisy, bright, overwhelming world.

I remember my sister asking, "When will it end?" And honestly, I don't think any of us knew. Because one day…it just did. No big shift. No miracle solution. The crying just started to ease.

Her baby grew more aware of the world and slowly, without us even noticing, the evenings became quieter.

Looking back now, my sister would tell you this: *It ends.* Eventually. It might feel endless when you're in it, like you're failing or missing something. But you're not. You're doing everything right. And the crying won't last forever.

So if you're deep in the witching hour right now, exhausted, doubting yourself, waiting for bedtime like it's the finish line, I want you to hear this clearly. You're not alone. And it will get easier.

If you are worried about your baby crying or it is continuous, it is always best to book an appointment with you GP or Health visitor to put your mind at ease and talk it over.

There's a particular cry that can rattle your bones like no other.

That red faced, full-bodied, inconsolable kind of cry that makes your heart race and your skin prickle.

If you've ever felt like you were about to snap, it's not because you're weak. It's because again, you're human. The sound embeds itself in your whole being.

Here's what's actually happening: when your baby cries, your cortisol levels spike. That's your body's stress hormone and it floods your system like a fire alarm going off. It's primal, your brain hears that sound and it reacts as if there's an emergency (because once upon a time, a crying baby was an emergency in the wild).

But the crazy part is that our nervous system doesn't know the difference between your baby crying because they're hungry…and your baby crying because there is a sabre-tooth tiger.

If you reach a point, a point where you feel stressed by it, it is fine to put your baby down somewhere safe and step away, even if they're still crying.

Let me say it again for the mother standing in the hallway with tears in her eyes and guilt in her throat.

It is okay to walk away for a minute or a few!

So what do you do?

You pause.

You breathe.

You put them somewhere safe, a cot, a Moses basket, a travel cot and you step away for 60 seconds, 90 seconds, however long you need to reset your system.

Even if they're still crying.

Because the most important thing in that moment is not perfection, it's safety. And that includes your safety too.

This doesn't make you a bad mum. This makes you a responsible one. A self-aware one. A strong one.

Crying won't break them.

But pushing yourself to the brink might.

Let's normalise saying, "*I'm at capacity.*"

Let's teach our children what self-regulation looks like by modelling it.

This is about caring so much that you recognise when your body is saying STOP.

You are not *just* a mum.

You are a nervous system, a heart, a body, a soul.

You matter.

So take the break. Put them down.

Reset.

They'll still be there.

But you'll be more grounded when you return.

MY BABY WILL CRY SOMETIMES.

Yep... they are communicating with you. Crying is part of the package deal!

I AM A GOOD PARENT AND I KNOW WHEN I NEED A BREAK

Try our 60 second reset! This is about calming your nervous system enough to get back in the game with a little steadiness.

Step 1: Drop your shoulders.

Seriously. Unclench your jaw too. Notice your fists? Uncurl them. Let your body know it's okay to soften.

Step 2: Breathe in for 4, hold for 4, out for 6.

It might feel silly at first. Do it anyway. Three rounds.

This slows your heart rate and signals your body that you're safe, even if your mind is racing.

Step 3: Ground through your senses.

Name: 5 things you can see...

4 things you can touch...
3 things you can hear...
2 things you can smell...
1 thing you like about yourself.

(Yes, this one is hard, but it matters.)

I AM A GOOD PARENT AND I KNOW WHEN I NEED A BREAK

Step 4: Say it out loud or in your head:

"This is hard, and I'm still doing my best. I am allowed to pause. I am safe. My baby is safe. I can come back to this."

WHAT EMOTIONS DO I FEEL WHEN MY BABY CRIES?

That's it. You did it!

Take a moment to pause and reflect. Whether you're in the thick of the witching hour, or remembering those early days, write freely about how it felt (or feels) to navigate your baby's crying.

Do you feel pressure to 'fix' it or stop it quickly? Where do you think that pressure comes from?

Can you offer yourself compassion in those moments, knowing that it's not your fault?

What small things help you stay grounded when things feel overwhelming?

CHAPTER EIGHTEEN

You're the expert. Trust yourself

There's something strange that happens the moment you grow a bump or cradle a newborn in your arms.

Everyone suddenly becomes a parenting expert.

Whether it's the woman behind you in the queue at the supermarket, your great aunt, or your well meaning but slightly overbearing neighbour, suddenly your baby's sleep, feeding, crying, outfit and nail length are up for public commentary.

"You should really put a hat on her."

"Have you tried winding him this way?"

"Oh, when I had babies we didn't do all that..."

And it's not just strangers. Family, friends and people you love start throwing in their twopence, usually with the best of intentions.

Your mum might remind you constantly how you were sleeping through the night at 6 weeks (spoiler: she's probably misremembering).

Your best friend might insist on a certain feeding schedule that worked wonders for her baby but makes you feel like you're doing it all wrong.

Here's the thing, they're not you. And it's not their baby.

Their experience is valid, yes. But so is yours. And that means you get to trust your gut.

That quiet, inner voice? The one that can tell between your baby's tired cry or their hungry cry (mostly)?

That little niggle when something doesn't feel right, even if everyone else says "*they're fine*!"

That's your superpower.

It can be hard at first, especially when you're tired, emotional and figuring it all out.

But the more you listen to that inner voice, the louder and more confident she becomes.

This chapter is giving you permission to nod, smile and then do what's best for you and your baby.

You don't have to justify your choices, explain your boundaries or apologise for doing things differently. If something doesn't sit right, you can say:

"Thanks, we're finding our own rhythm."

"That's interesting, I'll keep it in mind."

"We're doing what feels right for us."

You're not being rude.

You're protecting your space.

You're holding onto your peace.

You're trusting yourself.

And that, mama, is exactly what your baby needs.

Because nobody else in the world knows your baby the way you do.

I remember my friend telling me when she had her first baby she was sat in a cafe, baby in the sling, one boob out, sipping her cappuccino.

An older woman walked past and smiled…then paused.

"Oh love," she said, "you shouldn't let him sleep on you like that. You're making a rod for your own back."

She said, "thank you." But inside? Her heart sank.

In that moment that comment had her doubting herself. *Am I doing it wrong? Am I making things harder for the future me? Should I be putting him down?*

No she should not. I remember chatting it over later and saying to her, "Is what you're doing now working for you? Because if it's working for you, it's working."

And it was. It didn't matter if it wasn't in a book or on a schedule or *the way she used to do it.*

It was what they needed, right then. And that was enough.

Since then, I've lost count of how many times women in our classes have had to quietly reclaim their space, smiling, thanking people for their wisdom and then doing their own thing anyway.

Because parenting isn't a group project. It's about tuning into yourself. *Your* baby. *Your* rhythm.

I KNOW MY BABY!

You know more than you think.
And you are the expert here.

WRITE IT OUT

What does your baby like?	What doesn't your baby like?

THOUGHTS

EVERYTHING I LOVE ABOUT MY BABY

Use this space to be honest with what you've learnt since your baby was born.

CHAPTER NINETEEN

Routines, schedules and when they don't work

Ahhhh Googling the schedule?

If you've ever found yourself Googling, *baby schedule for 3 months and 4 days old*, welcome to the club.

We've all been there desperate for structure, some predictability, a little sliver of control in the chaos of early motherhood.

And the idea of a routine? Honestly, it sounds dreamy. A baby who naps like clockwork, eats every three hours and gives you a full night's sleep by 12 weeks.

We get sold this idea that if we just follow the right chart, buy the right white noise machine and commit to a schedule, our babies will settle down like obedient little bundles of joy.

But here's the thing no one really tells you…

Babies? They haven't read the books. They haven't been informed by Google.

They don't care that you've planned their nap at 10:00am. They're not interested in your colour coded schedule. They're tiny humans with developing brains, unpredictable bodies and zero concept of time.

Sometimes the routine will work like magic. Other days, it won't even touch the sides.

In fact, the pressure to force a routine that doesn't suit your baby or your family, can lead to more stress than it's worth.

One skipped nap and suddenly you're spiralling...*I've messed it all up, I'm failing, she'll never sleep again*, (she will).

It's okay to crave structure but it's also okay to let go of it sometimes.

This isn't about bashing routines. Routines can be amazing. They offer rhythm, a sense of safety and can absolutely help everyone feel more grounded.

But they should work for you, not the other way around. Flexibility isn't failure. It's motherhood.

You are allowed to have a plan...and change it.

You are allowed to want structure...and surrender to the chaos when needed.

You are allowed to build your days around your baby and build your baby's day around you when you need to.

You can try this:

Instead of strict times, I started following patterns, like feed, play, sleep.

I reminded myself that every phase ends, even the messy ones.

I stopped trying to *fix* my baby and started trusting that we'd figure it out together. I gave myself permission to rest, even if I really, really wanted to clean the kitchen.

Some days you'll feel like you've got it all flowing.

Other days will be held together by cold coffee and a lot of snacks.

Both are normal. Both are motherhood.

You're not a bad mum if the routine doesn't stick.

You're not lazy if you choose rest over structure. You're human.

You're doing great.

WHAT DAYS DO I LOVE?

Remember, it's not about having a perfect schedule. It's about creating a life that works for you and that can keep changing.

WHAT DOES AN 'IDEAL DAY' LOOK LIKE TO ME (EVEN IF IT FEELS OUT OF REACH RIGHT NOW)?

No pressure, just dream. What kind of flow would feel good for you and your baby?

WHAT PARTS OF MY DAY FEEL MOST STRESSFUL RIGHT NOW AND WHY?

Is it mornings, bedtime, feeding, juggling it all?

WHAT ROUTINES OR RHYTHMS (IF ANY) HAVE WORKED WELL FOR US SO FAR?

Even the small wins count. A pre nap cuddle, a coffee before they wake, 10 minutes of quiet.

When things don't go to plan, how do you usually respond? Do you feel guilt, frustration, defeat or do you adapt easily? There's no wrong answer.

CHAPTER TWENTY

Feed. And feed your way

If motherhood came with a scoreboard, feeding would be right at the top of the *things we feel judged for most* list.

Breast or bottle.

On demand or on schedule. Purees or baby-led. Pumping. Topping up. Formula guilt. Leaking through your bra. Crying because they won't latch. Crying because they will, but it hurts like hell. Crying because you stopped. Crying because you didn't.

Feeding isn't just feeding. It's loaded.

I remember it vividly with my first.

I really wanted to breastfeed. I thought I would.

No question about it, that was the plan. I had the lanolin cream and the breast pads and the willpower of a woman who'd read all the right things.

But then, she didn't latch. It wasn't even the toe-curling agony I had read about. I waited for the magic to kick in. It didn't.

And no one told me how bloody hard it could be. Or that support wouldn't be there when she actually needed to feed. Or that asking for help would feel like failure.

Let's just say it plainly: breastfeeding can be really hard. Not for everyone, but for so many of us.

The cracked nipples, the cluster feeding, the engorgement that makes you feel like your chest might explode. The constant second-guessing, *are they getting enough?*

Am I doing it right?

The pressure to enjoy it when all you feel is dread every time they start to root. The mental toll of being the only one who can feed them in the middle of the night when you're already hanging on by a thread.

It's a full time job with zero training, zero clock-off time and no guarantee it'll even go to plan. And yet we're told it's *natural.*

That it'll just happen. That it's free and easy. But no one talks about the pain, the loneliness or the feeling of being completely tethered.

This is the reality for so many women, and it deserves to be spoken about honestly, without guilt or sugar-coating.

Back to the story…eventually, '*I gave in*'.

Not because I didn't care, but because I did.

Because I needed her to eat. I needed to stop crying every time I fed her. I needed to function.

I remember being at a playgroup looking at all these mums sitting cross-legged on the play mats with their babies latched on like it was the most natural thing in the world.

They looked like Mother Earth, soft and glowing and calm (or that's how I saw it). And I was in the corner, panicking whether my bottle would still be warm enough for mid-morning. There was no fancy prep machine back then. Just a kettle, guesswork and a quiet prayer.

If I misjudged it? SHIT. Too hot.

Can't microwave it, something about hot spots?

So I'd cool it. Shake it. Panic. Heat. Re-cool. Repeat. Is it still ok for her? Now she's screaming blue murder at me.

But like with everything else in motherhood, eventually, you get into your rhythm.

You learn how to pack the bag. What works. What doesn't. You learn to trust yourself.

Still, that guilt? That mum guilt gremlin voice is back. It stuck with me.

Maybe that's why I breastfed my third until she was two.

I think some part of me still needed to prove that I could do it.

That I wasn't a failure. That I could meet that invisible gold standard of motherhood we all make up in our heads.

But here's the truth I've learnt after three babies and countless hours with women from all walks of life:

Feeding is not a performance.

It's nourishment.

It's love.

Whether it's from a breast or a bottle or a syringe or a cup.

You are feeding your baby.

You are doing it beautifully.

So here's what I want you to know:

- Breastfeeding isn't easy for everyone and if it's not working, it's not because you didn't try hard enough.
- Formula isn't failure. It's food. It's survival. It's sanity.
- You don't need to explain your choice to anyone.

- Stop when you want to stop. Not when the chart says. Not when your midwife raises an eyebrow. Not when your friend tells you her baby self-weaned at 4. You stop when it's right for you.

Fed is not just best. It's essential. It's enough. It's everything.

And to the mum still stuck in that fog, still crying into a muslin cloth at 2am thinking, *Why can't I do this?*

You are not alone. You're doing your best.

You are feeding your baby.

And that is more than enough.

So…feed.

And feed your way.

With love.

With courage.

With whatever works for you.

I FEED OUR WAY!

Feed the way that works for you.

Fed is best!

HOW DO I FEED MY BABY?

Simple question... how do you feed?

HOW DO I FEEL ABOUT THE WAY I FEED MY BABY?

Notes

CHAPTER TWENTY ONE

Ask for help before you hit a wall

I know what hitting the wall feels like.

It's not always dramatic. Sometimes it's subtle, the moment you forget where you left your car keys (again) or you find yourself staring into the fridge for a solid five minutes without knowing why.

Sometimes it's bursting into tears over burnt toast. Or silently resenting your partner for breathing too loudly.

The wall is real.

And motherhood, especially in the early days has a way of pushing us right up against it.

And yet, we hesitate to ask for help. Why?

Because we think we should be able to manage.

Because we don't want to be a burden.

Because we're scared people will think we're not coping.

Help looks different for everyone.

Try handing the baby to your partner and locking yourself in the bathroom for twenty uninterrupted minutes (even if you just scroll TikTok).

Or telling your mum, your sister, your best friend, you're not okay, instead of smiling and saying, "I'm fine."

Messaging a friend and saying, "Can you come over and just be here?"

Hiring a cleaner for a couple of hours if you can swing it or asking a friend to bring groceries.

You don't need to wait until you're running on empty.

You don't need to justify needing help.

You just need to be honest with yourself and with the people who love you.

Because when you ask for help before you hit the wall, something beautiful happens.

You remember that you're human.

You give others permission to support you.

And you show your children what it looks like to honour your needs.

That's not weakness. That's strength.

I know I work too much.

I know I put way too much pressure on myself.

I expect a ridiculous amount from myself, more than I would ever expect from anyone else.

And no, I'm not saying that just acknowledging you've hit the wall magically makes all those feelings disappear. It doesn't. But what it does do is open a door, a chance to understand yourself better. To look at what's driving that pressure. To explore what you really need, what you really want and what's stopping you from asking for help in the first place.

It's not easy work. But it is powerful work.

I had to start by being honest with myself. About how burnt out I felt.

About how often I said *"I'm fine"* when I was nowhere close to fine. And slowly I began to ask for help, not in a big dramatic way but in small, quiet ones. Like telling someone I was overwhelmed.

Like asking my partner to help clean the kitchen without feeling guilty about asking him.

And do you know what happened?

The world didn't fall apart.

People didn't think I was less capable.

And I didn't lose anything except the crushing pressure I'd put on myself to be everything to everyone.

HOW AM I, REALLY?

Go deeper than "I'm fine." What's sitting just under the surface?

WHAT ARE MY WARNING SIGNS THAT I AM APPROACHING MY LIMIT?

Think about physical signs, emotions, behaviours e.g. snapping more easily, forgetting things, feeling disconnected, headaches, etc.

WHAT WOULD SUPPORT ACTUALLY LOOK LIKE FOR ME RIGHT NOW?

Try to be specific: "An afternoon to myself", "Someone to cook dinner", "Childcare for an hour", "A friend to talk to".

Who could you reach out to for that support? (Remember: friends, family, professionals, online communities... your village is wider than you think.)

CHAPTER TWENTY TWO

Women v the world

Being a woman is not for the faint hearted.

Our lives move in cycles, not just the obvious, monthly kind that comes with period pains and mood swings but emotional, physical, hormonal waves that begin before we even understand them and never really stop.

One moment you're fine, maybe even thriving and the next you're staring into space wondering how you ended up in a life where everyone seems to expect something from you and you're still trying to figure out who you are.

And yes, there are times where it feels like it's you against the world.

From puberty to postnatal recovery to menopause and everything in between, our bodies and minds are constantly shifting.

Up and down, peaking and troughing like we're on a rollercoaster we never signed up for. One minute you're full of energy, ideas, motivation and the next? You want to cancel everything, burn it all down and hide under a blanket (maybe with a sharer Dairy Milk).

And here's the thing nobody tells you loud enough. It's okay to feel resentful sometimes.

Yes, even towards the people you love.

Especially when it feels like your whole world has shifted and theirs hasn't moved an inch.

Maybe it's your partner who still gets up and goes to work like nothing happened while you're at home bleeding, leaking, healing and pretending to be fine. Maybe it's friends who seem blissfully unaware of how heavy life feels for you right now. Maybe it's society because, let's be honest, most of this wasn't designed with us in mind.

That resentment? That frustration? That moment when you think, *why am I the one holding it all?*

It doesn't make you selfish. It makes you honest.

We've been conditioned to brush it off. To say, *"I'm fine",* when you're anything but. To feel guilty for wanting time alone or snapping when you're touched out, exhausted and just done.

But your feelings are valid. Full stop.

They are signs. Messages. And if you ignore them, they don't disappear but bury themselves deeper until they explode somewhere else.

So let them out.

Cry if you need to. Rant to a friend. Write down the messy stuff that you'd never say out loud. Speak your truth, even if it's uncomfortable. Your emotions are not an inconvenience, they're a compass. And ignoring them doesn't make you strong, it just makes you silent.

You're allowed to take up space.

You're allowed to feel what you feel whether that's rage, joy, sadness, love, resentment, hope, all of it.

You're allowed to fall apart and rebuild yourself again and again.

Because that's what we do.

We live in rhythms. Our bodies tell stories every single month of release, renewal, rebuilding. Of everything we carry, everything we give. And yeah, sometimes we get sick of it.

That's okay too.

But don't ever believe you're too much. Or not enough.

So if today feels heavy, if your chest is tight with unspoken words, if you're scrolling social media and feeling bitter that someone else gets to just go to the gym without planning the logistics of an international summit to get out the door, I see you.

You're not alone.

You're a woman.

And that, my fierce warrior, is a bloody powerful thing to be, even when it's hard.

I AM A SUPERWOMAN.

Yes you are... even when it is hard and you feel like you're carrying the world!

WHAT THINGS HAVE I FELT RESENTFUL ABOUT RECENTLY?

Be honest, these are your pages. Maybe it is having to be home with a baby? Not going to work? Being the one who has to organise life? Being the default parent?

WHAT DO I FEEL RESENTFUL ABOUT AND WHY?

Can you identify one main thing you feel resentful about?

Use this circle to try to understand why you feel resentful

Who or what is it connected to? What would you say if you could speak that truth freely? Without guilt, without apology.

CHAPTER TWENTY THREE

The evolution of women

It's mind-boggling to think that just 100 years ago, women didn't even have the right to vote.

Our roles were clearly mapped out.

Men earned the money.

Women kept the house.

End of. There was order. Simplicity. Predictability, even if it came at the cost of freedom, identity and equality.

Fast forward to now and women are everywhere, running businesses, leading companies, juggling families, making bold choices. And I *love* it!

We've evolved. The women before us fought for that evolution. We didn't get here by accident, we got here through sheer grit, blood, tears and the stubborn refusal to settle for less.

But here's a question I ask myself…

Have men evolved at the same pace?

Now, before anyone gets defensive, let me say this, I'm not generalising all men. I know incredible partners (my husband included) who pull their weight and then some.

But I've also spoken to hundreds of women and this is a hot topic that keeps bubbling up in the background.

Because something changes when you become a mum.

Your whole identity shifts. You go from being you, the woman, the partner, the worker to being Mum. Centre of the household. CEO of nappies, meal plans, emotional regulation, doctor appointments, social calendars, washing rotation and birthday cards.

And your partner? Lovely as they may be. Do they experience that same shift?

Often, the answer is *no*. Their world keeps ticking in a straight line, while yours detours off road with no map, full of mud, chaos and nappy bags that somehow smell even when they're empty.

We are constantly adjusting, constantly morphing into new versions of ourselves.

That's evolution.

But evolution isn't always graceful. Sometimes it's chaotic.

Sometimes, it's realising that the role you've grown into doesn't come with clear instructions, just an endless mental 'to do' list and no time to wee alone.

And while we're on the topic of roles, can we just talk about the universal dread of deciding what's for tea?

Nobody warned me that one of adulthood's biggest stressors would be trying to answer the question…

What are we having for tea?

Honestly, I was not made to be a homemaker. If I lived in the 1940s, I would have been a domestic disaster.

Give me a funnel set up, a Mailchimp campaign, a Canva graphic and I'm away.

But put me in front of a fridge with ingredients. I freeze.

My worst (or best) parenting meal moment? '*Picky Bits Tea*'.

That's what we called it. A little plate of total randomness. Raisins, apple slices, cheese chunks, dry cereal, crackers, cucumber sticks, the last of the ham and that one spoonful of coleslaw that's just slightly fizzy.

To me? Failure.

To my kids? Culinary genius.

When they did a school project and wrote about their favourite meal at home, all three of them said '*Picky Bits Tea*'. Who knew, maybe I would make a homemaker after all!

Here I was thinking I was not up to scratch on these homely tasks, when in their eyes, I'd created a fun meal that they actually looked forward to.

That's the thing about evolution. You don't always notice you're getting it right because you're too busy measuring yourself against outdated expectations.

We're not living in our grandmother's world anymore.

We are navigating careers, motherhood, mental load, hormones, ambition, relationships and personal growth all in a single day.

Maybe men and women haven't both evolved at the same pace but being open, honest and willing to talk about what we need, what we carry and what roles we're each stepping into is the first real step toward something more balanced, more supportive and a hell of a lot more human.

We're carving out paths while still wondering what to cook, remembering it's school fancy dress tomorrow and trying to act like we have it all together when half the time we just want five minutes to breathe.

So no, we're not the women of 1924.

We're the women of now.

Of change.

Of choice.

Of imperfect, brilliant, multitasking magic.

I AM A WOMAN OF CHOICE.

Yes you are!

WRITE DOWN EVERYTHING I'M CARRYING RIGHT NOW. THE DAILY, WEEKLY, MONTHLY TASKS THAT FILL UP MY MIND AND MY TIME

From the packed lunches and washing piles to remembering birthday cards and booking appointments. Big things, small things, invisible things.

I've given you plenty of room... I know you by now. Use the next few pages to list it all out!

MORE THINGS I AM CARRYING

Is there anything on that list you could pass to a partner, a family member, a friend?

Could a teenager in your neighbourhood earn a bit of pocket money washing your car or helping tidy up the garden? Could you stretch to a cleaner once a month?

Even one small handover can make a big difference.

Write it out on the next page. Circle what's essential. Put a big star next to the things you could share and start a plan to do it.

Because your energy is valuable. And so are you. Use these pages to simply write it out in order of importance.

List it below in order of importance.

CHAPTER TWENTY FOUR

My story

If I'm honest, this book wasn't something I sat down and strategically planned to write.

It started as scribbled notes in my diary at 3am while going over what women have told me in classes.

I felt overwhelmed in recent years, building a business and raising 3 children but didn't want to *bother* anyone.

I sent messages to friends that began with, *is it just me or...?*

Because that's the thing. For a long time, I did think it was just me.

Even though I had incredible people around me, even though I loved my children more than anything, I couldn't shake this quiet, nagging feeling that I was slowly losing bits of myself in the whirlwind of parenthood.

And no one had really warned me about that. No one told me that the hardest part wouldn't be the sleepless nights or the cluster feeds but the identity shift. The guilt. The constant second-guessing.

What I craved wasn't more advice. It wasn't more checklists or milestone apps.

I wanted honesty. Connection.

I wanted to hear someone say, "Hey, I've been there and you're doing better than you think."

That yearning, along with the birth of my own babies, eventually gave life to BabyBeats.

Creating BabyBeats wasn't just about launching a business. It was about building a space for women, one where they could move their bodies, connect with their babies and most importantly, reconnect with themselves. Over the years, I've had the honour of speaking to hundreds of women, each with their own story, each with their own fears, strengths, doubts and dreams.

And let me tell you, those conversations have changed me.

They've shaped how I see motherhood. Not as one size fits all, not as picture perfect but as powerful, complex, emotional, real.

They've taught me that behind every pushchair is a woman doing her absolute best even when she's questioning every move.

They've shown me that community matters. That we need more women cheering for women. That being a woman's woman is one of the most radical and beautiful things we can be.

So this book is that too, a cheerleader in paper form. A friend on the bookshelf.

You're not alone.

I didn't want to write another parenting manual filled with *should* and *must*. I wanted to create something that didn't just talk about motherhood but talked to women.

Something you could pick up in your dressing gown, with one hand holding a brew and feel seen. Something that tells the truth without the doom, that reminds you how strong, soft, messy and magical you are even when you don't feel it.

Writing this book has been healing for me.

If reading it gives even one woman the permission to breathe, to laugh, to let go of the pressure or to feel less alone, then it's done its job.

You won't have found perfection in these pages. You'll have found that even when it feels like you've lost yourself, you're still there.

And she's worth finding again.

Thank you for holding this book in your hands.

Thank you for being part of this story too.

We're in this together.

I WANT TO ATTEND A CLASS MYSELF!

Want to attend a Baby Beats class with your little one? Or maybe a fun-filled toddler session? Perhaps you're craving a class that's just for you, to move, to breathe to reconnect.

Wherever you're at in your motherhood journey, there's a place for you at BabyBeats.

No pressure, no judgement, just movement and a moment to feel like you again.

Come as you are...
classes running
nationwide.
We'll meet you there.
Scan the code to find
your local class.

WANT SOME FREE STUFF?

Always!!! We've got you covered.

Whether you're looking for simple guides to help re engage your core after birth, gentle massage routines to help your little one (and you!) sleep better or just something that makes this stage feel a little less overwhelming, you can download it all, totally free, right here.

Because support should never come with a price tag.
Scan the code to get some lovely free stuff!

Gremlin Not Included

CONCLUSION

Embrace your unique journey

If you've made it to this final chapter, firstly, thank you. Truly. Thank you for showing up, not just for this book but for yourself.

Thank you for being open to the messy middle of motherhood, for daring to look beneath the surface of 'I'm fine' and explore what's really going on. That takes courage.

There is no one *'right way'* to do motherhood.

There's only *your* way.

Your version. *Your* rhythm. *Your* voice.

Motherhood is not a straight line, it's a winding, wobbly, zigzag of a path. One minute you feel like you've got it all under control and the next you're Googling, *how long can a human survive on three hours of sleep and cold toast?*

That's real. That's normal. That's you doing it.

I hope that through these pages, you've found something that made you feel seen. Maybe a chapter made you laugh. Maybe one made you cry. Maybe one gave you the permission you didn't know you needed.

And I hope, above all, that you've realised there is no finish line to reach. You don't need to *get back* to the old you because the woman you're becoming is worth knowing too.

And in those moments where you feel like you've lost yourself, know that you haven't. You're just evolving. You're growing right alongside your baby.

This isn't just a chapter in your motherhood story.

It's *your* story. And *you* get to write it *your* way.

ACKNOWLEDGEMENTS

It is all about the people

Mum, a huge thank you for proofreading everything I've ever written. As someone with dyslexia, the idea of writing a book once felt impossible. But you've been my extra pair of eyes, my quiet confidence and your help has been absolutely invaluable.

To my sister, thank you for being my sounding board, my honest critic and the person who always tells it like it is (even when you think something is utter rubbish). Your input has made this book so much better. Sisters always.

To my children, thank you for adapting to the chaos of Mum working day and night, juggling qualifications, writing programmes and somehow writing a book in the middle of it all. I'll never forget the times you hid under my desk during meetings or whispered "are you finished yet?" from behind the laptop. You've been patient, kind and totally amazing. I love you all unconditionally.

Dad, thank you for the never ending tax advice, business translations and for walking the dog for me when I was busy. I know you love it as much as him. And to my brother… thanks for being born. You're welcome, by the way. It's because I wasn't that bad that Mum and Dad had you.

To my friends and family, thank you for showing up, for being brutally honest when I needed it and for cheering me on every step of the way. Extra special shout outs to Helen and Uncle Jim for your support, laughter and letting me rant!

To my animals, your weirdness brings me joy daily.

And finally, to my husband, my biggest cheerleader. Thank you for believing in me, encouraging me and never once telling me to slow down. Your unwavering faith in me has meant the world.

This book exists because you never let me believe I couldn't.

DEDICATED TO THE MEMORY OF BRADLEY KILNER

This book has touched on many emotions and feelings that new parents, women and men everywhere may face.

No matter how heavy things feel, support is always within reach. You matter. It is not failure to ask for support.

If you ever need someone to lean on, the resources listed below are just some of the incredible charities and organisations ready to help.

TOMMY'S – WWW.TOMMYS.ORG

NATIONAL CHILDBIRTH TRUST (NCT) –WWW.NCT.ORG.UK

ACTION FOR CHILDREN –WWW.ACTIONFORCHILDREN.ORG.UK

DAD MATTERS UK – WWW.DADMATTERS.ORG.UK

ANDY'S MAN CLUB – WWW.ANDYSMANCLUB.CO.UK

SAMARITANS – WWW.SAMARITANS.ORG

MIND – WWW.MIND.ORG.UK

PANDAS FOUNDATION –
WWW.PANDASFOUNDATION.ORG.UK

About the Author

Rose's movement journey began as a dancer, where she discovered a lifelong love for the way the body moves, adapts and changes through every stage of life. From there, she stepped into the world of fitness, teaching everything from spinning to body pump before specialising in pre- and postnatal fitness and sports therapy.

As the founder of the multi-award-winning programmes BabyBeats, Mindful Movers, Before Birth and Functional Foundations, Rose has been featured in The New York Journal, BBC and Women's Health Magazine. Her programmes have supported thousands of women across the UK, helping them regain strength, confidence and connection with their bodies through pregnancy, postpartum recovery and every stage of womanhood.

Not only have her programmes transformed lives on a personal level, they're also taught by instructors nationwide and officially endorsed by EMD UK, the governing body for group exercise.

Rose is deeply passionate about making movement simple, adaptable, and empowering because women already juggle enough. She believes motherhood should never mean choosing between career and family, and champions the idea that women can (and should) have both. A strong advocate for female entrepreneurship, she encourages women to build businesses that are meaningful, empowering and flexible around family life.

Beyond her professional work, Rose is a proud mum of three, an animal lover (with two cats and a dog) and at her happiest outdoors exploring on long walks with her husband.

With Love

GLOSSARY OF TERMS

Cortisol -The *Oh my God everything is on fire* hormone. Rises when your baby cries, when your toast burns or when you hear "Mummyyyyyy" for the 274th time before 9am. Not evil, just your body trying to help. But too much? You'll feel like a fizzing bottle of cola. Breathe, rest, repeat.

Decision Fatigue - The reason you can't choose what to watch on Netflix or what's for tea. Your brain has made 14,000 micro decisions today, including - but not limited to - which socks are clean, how to respond to a tantrum and whether it's right or left boob next.

Survival Mode - It's the setting your body slips into when you're running on snacks and you're doing the bare minimum to keep tiny humans alive. That is more than enough.

Matrescence - The very real and very un-talked about transformation you go through when you become a mother. Like adolescence but with more nappies, less sleep and nobody telling you it's normal to feel totally undone.

Adolescence - You remember this one? Spotty, moody, confusing. Just to refresh your memories.

Hustle Culture -The ridiculous idea that if you're not working, grinding, side-hustling or *building an empire* 24/7, you're failing. Spoiler: You're not. Resting is rebellious. Napping is productive. You don't need to monetise your hobbies. Breathe.

Picky Bits Tea Recipe - Not an actual recipe. Just the sacred, family saving meal of bits. Cheese. Cucumber. Crackers. Maybe some hummus if you're feeling wild. The dinner you make when cooking feels like a personal attack. Raid the fridge, if it's not walking, it's fair game!

Abdominals - Yes, you have them. These are a collection of muscles that help with just about everything, the *six-pack* muscles are included in these.

Mood Ring - If you were born in the '80s you know this vibe. If you weren't don't worry, they'll be back in fashion any day now (mark my words). It was the ultimate accessory, a plastic gem that 'read your mood' and turned weird colours depending on your emotional state (or the room temperature). Wore it. Loved it. Turned your finger green. Genius.

Printed in Dunstable, United Kingdom

68413388R00127